A Guidebook for Course Development and Evaluation

For the Classroom and Online

2nd edition

Rick Upchurch

Tools to Lead Publishing

A GUIDEBOOK FOR CURRICULUM DEVELOPMENT AND ASSESSMENT:
FOR THE CLASSROOM AND ONLINE 2ND EDITION

Copyright © 2019 by Rick Upchurch: rlupchurch@gmail.com

Published by Tools to Lead Publishing

Printed in the United States of America

ISBN: 978-0-9833239-5-2

TABLE OF CONTENTS

CHAPTER 1 - INTRODUCTION

This book is specifically designed for the individual who has been charged with preparing and teaching a course, or for those charged with developing curriculum. It is focused on the pragmatic application of course development principles to designing an effective course. The material in this book will be an invaluable aid for improving the quality and functionality of any curriculum. While the material in this book may apply to any teaching experience, it is primarily focused on those teaching college level courses. Because of that, this book focuses on the practical, i.e. designing and evaluating curriculum for the effectiveness of its goal: student learning.

Unfortunately, the fact of the matter is that most of those teaching in higher education have received little or no instruction about HOW to teach. They are usually experts in their subject matter, yet approach the teaching task armed only with the experiences they themselves have had in the classroom. In some cases those experiences have provided insight into effective learning, but as often as not they provide memories of methods and practices to avoid. A majority of college instructors' default in their teaching style to the methods by which they have been taught, without regard to whether or not this is the most effective method of instruction, and often without an awareness, that other methods even exist.

Part of the problem faced in this scenario is the lack of a personal educational philosophy that clearly describes the intent of the instructional process. To put this in the simplest terms: is the instruction to be an impartation of knowledge by a properly prepared and credentialed instructor, or is the focus on the acquisition of knowledge by the student? This is the classic "sage on the stage" versus "guide on the side" debate. On the surface, this disparity might seem to be the same thing, but consider this, in the first case, the instructor's job is to make sure the material is covered at a sufficient depth to qualify as a "college" level course. While it is hoped that the students understand the material and are able to integrate the knowledge, in "the sage on the stage" model, that is not the most important consideration. *The most important consideration for this model is covering the assigned material.*

In the second case, "guide on the side" model, the emphasis is upon student learning. This does not necessarily mean covering less material, but does mean covering the material in a way that students grasp the concepts and are able to integrate the knowledge more fully into their personal gestalt. This model requires more than subject matter knowledge; it requires effort in determining which teaching methods should be used to most effectively communicate the information so that student learning occurs. It also requires a basic knowledge of learning styles, e.g. visual, auditory, kinesthetic, reading/writing. *Without negating the importance of the instructor and his/her credentials, the focus of this model is squarely on the student and their learning.*

This philosophical perspective is a crucial one. This perspective should be addressed by at least the Division Chair, and preferably by the Academic Dean or Provost. Once the educational philosophy of the institution (or division) is clearly articulated, then comes the task of educating those who teach at that institution (or in that division) about the ramifications of the philosophy upon the everyday practice of teaching. The educational philosophy should also touch upon the basics that are held dear by the faculty, and may even distinguish the institution. For instance, one school will determine that every graduate will have had the instruction and experience of delivering multiple public presentations so there is an expected competency in this area. Another institution will focus on "writing across the curriculum" with the expected competency that every student will be able to write at a certain established level.

Each institution will, ideally, make decisions about what is part of its philosophy and clearly articulate this in a statement of philosophy. This statement will then be used in their conversations about curriculum and in the design of the curriculum. Where the institution/division has not invested in this process, or does not consider it a priority, the burden falls back to the instructor to determine a personal educational philosophy, which will guide her teaching, both in preparation and in delivery.

Questions that can be used to start this conversation include:

- What does "college level" education mean?
- What values do our institution uphold relative to the teaching process?
- Rank the current focus of the institution regarding its educational philosophy with Faculty Focused at one end of the continuum and Student Focused at the other. What has brought this institution to this place? Where do we as an institution want to be on this scale? Why?
- Should there be any variance in these perspectives relative to one department/course over another, e.g. chemistry vs. philosophy.

THE PROBLEM

Most syllabi, let alone a complete curriculum, do not go through a standardized review process to ensure an acceptable level of quality. That may seem surprising, even shocking but it is true. For those who teach in the traditional classroom there is often no evaluation of the syllabi or discussion of curricular issues. For adult degree programs, or online programs, there is typically a curriculum development process, but in most cases, it does not include a qualitative analysis of the curriculum against the institution's educational philosophy and best practices. In best-case scenarios, the curriculum is written by subject matter experts using a template with agreed upon pieces already inserted in an approved format. In some cases the curriculum is reviewed by an administrator who may not have the time and/or understanding needed to evaluate the quality of the curriculum. In the worst case, Subject Matter Experts (SME) are simply asked to write a course with little or no guidance about what that should look like or how it fits into the overall academic program. Perhaps there is an old syllabus to go by, but little guidance is given, or available, to the course writer, since everyone is already too busy trying to develop his or her own course. Even where a template is provided, there is a great deal of variation from institution to institution and sometimes even within an institution about what are considered the most important ingredients of a well-written curriculum.

Here are some of the problems I have observed:

- No template provided, or only the barest framework – this allows the SME the greatest amount of freedom to design the course as they choose. Unfortunately, the implication is that there are no boundaries when in fact there *are* boundaries; they are simply unwritten. Without a template of any kind, SME can feel deserted and alone at one end of the continuum, or all-powerful at the other. In this situation, connections between course objectives and the course material are often inconsistent. For adult programs which depend on consistency of format for better student interaction/retention, this model represents unique challenges in program integrity and achievement of outcomes at every level.

- No attempt to evaluate homework for load or an absence of guidelines related to appropriate load – this may sound trivial but one of the greatest complaints students have is that some weeks the homework is too heavy and other weeks the homework is almost non-existent. What is an appropriate load related to homework assignments? Included in this consideration is the reality that few faculty understand how to balance their homework assignments relative to the institution's philosophy of education or other expectations – many of which may be unwritten.

- No guidance as to how to write appropriate course objectives – the ability to write effective course objectives is often overlooked, especially by new faculty. These course objectives, if well written, can direct the flow of the course like the banks of a river guide the water to the ocean. Appropriately, written course objectives support the objectives of the program and the institution as a whole. The course becomes part of a whole garment that is tailored to fit the mission of the institution and the needs of the student.

- No attempt to evaluate homework against course objectives.

- No attempt to evaluate homework against an accepted learning model.

- No attempt to evaluate learning activities against course objectives.

- Little or no attempt to evaluate learning activities against an accepted learning model.

- Little or no attempt to evaluate learning activities against appropriate educational methodology.

- No clear explanation of how the objectives of the course can be measured for success.

- For faith-based institutions, there is a misunderstanding of faith integration, which is either superficial or ignored.

THE SOLUTION

The premise used in this guidebook is an educational philosophy based on a student-learning model. The material found herein will look at practical ways an instructor can design a course to enhance the likelihood that student learning takes place. Using this guidebook will equip the course writer to be more effective in avoiding the pitfalls, which are part of the higher education landscape, and, more importantly, provide students with a superior educational experience.

The impetus for this guidebook comes from developing a tool, which addresses the concerns raised above. That tool is the U-CAT or Upchurch Curriculum Audit Tool or the U-CATO for online courses. The U-CAT allows the writer to evaluate a course against various standards. Using the information from the U-CAT the course developer can focus on relevant areas and develop a more integrated and balanced curriculum. With this tool, the writer can spot at a glance any problem areas and then address the problem. The use of this tool is crucial for anyone who is writing a new course or modifying an existing one. The U-CAT can also be an invaluable aide in evaluating curriculum. It is a tool, which has value for the novice as well as the experienced course writer. Administrators can use the U-CAT to review curriculum relative to the institution's educational philosophy and other expectations.

The Curriculum Audit is described in detail later in this guidebook and available free electronically by download. Please feel free to modify the UCAT or the UCATO to meet the needs of your institution.

https://sites.google.com/site/toolstolead/in-the-news/UCAT

The balance of the guidebook will look at the topics below. Each of the topics below and their relevance for curriculum development and assessment will be examined. The differences between curriculums delivered in the classroom and online will be discussed, with the differences noted.

- The Course Description – start with the end in mind
- Course Objective (learning outcomes)
- A Taxonomy for Learning
- Assignments
- Learning Activities
- Instructional style
- Assessment
- Faith Integration
- Calculating Seat Time
- Curriculum Audit

CHAPTER 2 - THE COURSE DESCRIPTION

The Course Description (CD) is what the student sees in the catalog and often is the deciding factor in whether or not to take the course. The inclusion of the CD in the catalog provides a type of "agreement" between the student and the institution that should not be taken lightly. Often, student's remark in the post-class evaluation, complaining about the lack of direct connection between the CD and what was actually covered in the course. It is wise, therefore, to focus upon clearly understanding the course description BEFORE starting work on the course design. It is important to examine the CD carefully and even to dissect the CD a bit in order to probe the full implications of the description. The CD provides the boundaries for the course, and those boundaries must be observed to avoid problems and possible challenges. If for some reason the CD is no longer in line with the division/institution's needs, there is almost certainly an approved process by which it can be modified. However, such modifications can often take weeks if not months to take effect, meaning that, regardless of the instructor/writer's inclinations, the course may have to be taught from the basis of the existing CD in the short-run.

In the case where the CD has not been written, it is wise to write the CD in such a way that it is descriptive without placing too many constrictions upon the course. This can allow for easier modification as the course evolves without the hassle of going through a change process. Here is an example of a CD, which demonstrates the point above:

Well Written:	Poorly Written:
Philosophy of Religion - Study and discussion of a broad range of issues in the philosophy of religion, such as religious epistemology, the ontological argument, the cosmological argument, the teleological argument, religion and science, and the problem of evil.	**Philosophy of Religion** – A consideration of various attempts to provide a philosophical formulation and defense of the basic tenets of the theistic worldview, with particular attention to recent analytic philosophy.

In the well-written example, the inclusion of "such as" leaves room for the course to be easily modified while at the same time giving a sense of what the course will cover. In the poorly written example, the words "theistic" and "recent analytical philosophy" reflect a too narrow focus, which is out of line with the title of the course, in that the scope of "Philosophy of Religion", is a much broader topic than the proposed focus.

Here are three things to keep in mind when writing a CD:

1. The course title should be reflected in the course description. This may seem obvious but too many times the course description does not seem to have anything to do with the title, confusing the students and affecting the integrity of the catalog, and possibly the institution.

2. The course description should contain enough particulars to allow the reader to get a feel for what the course will cover, without being too specific. There needs to be room in the CD for some latitude on the part of the instructor teaching the course and still fulfill the CD.

3. The course description should be written in a style, which, ideally, would entice the reader to enroll in the course, keeping in mind the two points above. Styles evolve but a good rule of thumb is to match the complexity of the course description to the course level. For instance, a freshman course would have less technical jargon and be written in a more accessible style than a senior level course.

Here is another example of a course description:

Advanced Organizational Behavior: This course investigates the importance and impact of individual and organizational behavior upon the culture, climate, and structure of an organization. The practical application of human resource theories in the organization is introduced, emphasizing the relevance of the theories to contemporary events.	Advanced Organizational Behavior: A course designed to develop an understanding of behavioral concepts for effective management of organization. Topics include theories related to work environment, group dynamics, motivation, leadership, and organizational change strategies.

Which of the course descriptions above best stays within the guideline suggested? Why?

CHAPTER 3 - COURSE OBJECTIVE (LEARNING OUTCOMES)

The inclusion of Course Objectives is often viewed by some as one of those things required by administrators, which has little or no value to the course itself. This is an unfortunate perspective as the course objectives, if well written, can be effectively used to guide the development of the curriculum, making it more focused and effective. *The secret here is that for this to happen, the course objectives have to be well written.* The writing of course objectives requires the ability to step away from the proximity of the trees to get a clear view of the forest. When viewed from this perspective, the objectives should have a holistic feel, identifying the learning that should occur because of completing the course, which stays true to the course description.

How does one write an effective course objective? The secret is in two parts. The first part has to do with understanding the concept of the "irreducible minimum." The "irreducible minimum" is a concept proposed by Bruce Wilkinson in his book *The Seven Laws of the Learner*. He says that in any course, some of the content is more important than other parts, i.e. there is some learning that is crucial to the successful completion of the course. Wilkinson would say this applies not only to the *design* of the course objectives but also equally to the actual class *sessions*.

The ability to categorize the expected learning into from four to six statements provides a focus, which effectively steers the curriculum through the maze of information deluge. Unfortunately, this sounds easier than it may actually be. I have seen lists of up to 20 different course objectives proposed by course writers who genuinely believed that each one of the objectives were crucial to the course. There are two things, which happen in cases like this; either the learning is so shallow and/or fragmented that little is actually retained, or the 20 objectives are, in reality, sub points under four to six comprehensive objectives. If the first is true, then the course writer needs to be counseled as to the reality of what is actually doable within the course boundaries. In this case, the homework load area of the U-CAT can be an invaluable guide to demonstrate that too much is being required. If the second is true, then it is just a matter of grouping the terms and writing course objectives, which are less specific but accomplish the same goals.

The second part has to do with the choice of words used to compose the course objective. It might seem as if this, also, is an exercise easily accomplished, but that is misleading. I would have to say that composing clear, measurable course objectives is an area where most course writers struggle. There are several considerations, which go into the choice of words used to formulate an effective course objective.

Here are some basic principles

- Have an action word that describes what the student will *do* differently because of your course.

- Describe meaningful learning.
- Be measured/verified; i.e., you can measure students' ability to achieve them.
- Represent high levels of thinking, rather than trivial tasks.
- Be written in plain language students can understand.

Probably the best way to do this is to have a list of appropriate action words beside you as you are writing the objectives. I highly recommend using terms from the taxonomy listed in the next section when composing the course objectives. Words such as the following have been found to be good choices when developing course objectives:

Construct	Critique
Summarize	Communicate
Explain	Classify
Analyze	Compare
Differentiate	Articulate
Organize	Evaluate
Define	Understand

One word of caution here: Some institutions frown on the use of the word "understand" in course objectives since it is notoriously difficult to evaluate exactly what anyone truly "understands."

Objectives for the course are typically introduced with a statement such as "Upon completion of this course the student should be able to:" The use of the word "should" is debated by some who believe a better choice is "will." The difference is significant. When using "should" the objective can be evaluated but there is no expectation that in each case the learning is guaranteed. Using the word "will" places a much greater burden on the teaching/learning process as it asserts that the student will be able to be positively evaluated as to their successful achievement of the stated objective. I urge institutions to use "should" unless there is a strong curricular and assessment process in place, which can address discrepancies.

Whether "should," "will," or some other term is employed, the course objectives listed under this statement describe the focus on the learning, which is planned for that course. For example, a course on Adult Development and Life Assessment could have the following objectives:

> Upon successful completion of this course, adult learners should be able to:
>
> 1. articulate personal worldview assumptions and relate those assumptions to life and career development
> 2. demonstrate knowledge and application of classical and contemporary adult development theory
> 3. demonstrate awareness of personal strengths and relate those strengths to life and career development
> 4. demonstrate confidence in anticipating and managing adult transitions through lifelong learning

Let us see how these fulfill the requirements for effective course objectives:

> First, does each of the objectives have an action word that describes what the student will DO differently because of completing the course? The action words used are "articulate" and "demonstrate." Although there is possibly too much dependence upon the word "demonstrate,"

the objectives clearly indicate, what the student should be able to "do differently" because of the course.

Second, do the objectives describe meaningful learning? For objective #1, the students will have to have become aware of their personal worldview and how that relates to their life goals – this seems to be meaningful learning. For objective #2 the students will become aware of adult learning theory and will have to demonstrate that awareness. Since this class is designed for adults, the acquisition of that knowledge should conceivably assist the student in future learning endeavors: again, this seems like meaningful learning. For objective #3 the students will demonstrate an awareness of their personal strengths, especially as they relate to their career and personal development. Anytime a student becomes more self-aware and can demonstrate how that awareness can affect their life, it should be considered as meaningful learning. For objective #4 the expectation is that the students will be able to demonstrate confidence and anticipation in managing adult transitions through lifelong learning. This objective may not describe meaningful learning unique to the other objectives and could, be combined with objective #2. Additionally, this fourth objective will be difficult to measure as to whether or not it has been achieved, which is the next point.

Third, the objectives should be able to be measured/verified; i.e., you can measure students' ability to achieve them. This kind of assessment can be designed for the first three objectives in the example but not for the fourth objective.

Fourth and finally, the objectives should represent high levels of thinking, rather than trivial tasks. All four objectives qualify under this guideline.

Outcome statements that meet all of the above criteria are sometimes challenging to craft alone. A good practice is to collaborate with a peer or Department Chair/Dean when crafting course objectives. With practice, you should be able to get your ideas down to a few clearly written statements that define the purpose of the course for you and your students.

There is a place on the U-CAT for the course objectives to be listed along with an associated code letter which, which will be explained in detail later.

WEEKLY LEARNING OBJECTIVES

Although not specifically connected to the U-CAT, a well written course will not only have course objectives which span the learning for the entire course, but will also have weekly learning objectives, think of them as tactical units, which support and contribute to achieving the course objectives. There are usually about 2 – 4 weekly objectives, but can be as many as 8 – 10 depending upon the length of the class session. These objectives provide the boundaries into which the river of learning should flow for the duration of a specific class session. When developing the course, the first step after the completion of the course objectives would be to map those objectives over the duration of the course, using a sequencing model.

Think of a sequencing model as the strategic plan to accomplish the course objectives. As with any strategic plan, there are individual, tactical, goals, which lead in an organized fashion to the accomplishment of the overall plan (course objectives). The sequencing model can come from personal experience, the textbook, etc. Its purpose is to guide the student through the material in a manner, which fosters learning and fulfills the promise of the course objectives. The mapping of the course objectives onto this model allows the course writer to make sure nothing is missed. In some cases, a course objective will be connected to one week while another course objective may show up connected to every week. *The important thing is that each objective connects somewhere.* Using the example above of the Adult Development and Life Assessment course and a sequencing model based on following the structure of the textbooks, which will be used in the course, a reasonable map would look like the diagram below. Note that while only two sessions, or class meetings, are mentioned in the example, the principle needs to be repeated, with each session objective mapped back to a course objective:

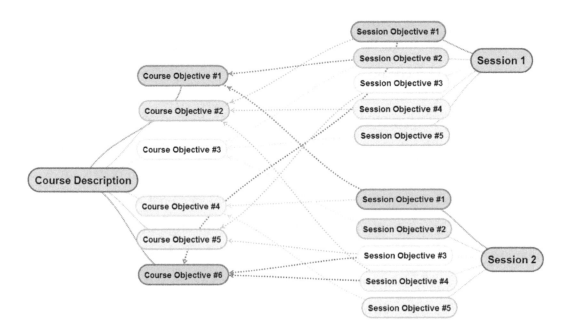

The weekly learning objectives should be relatively few in number and written in a similar fashion as the course objectives, except focused on achieving the learning targeted for that specific class session.

For example, the course objectives for a course in Biblical Covenants might be:

> Upon completion of this course, the students should be able to:
> 1. Define covenant, the various types of biblical covenants and their significance.
> 2. Describe the major points of the key biblical covenants: Abrahamic, Mosaic, Davidic, and New.
> 3. Communicate God's redemptive nature and acts using biblical examples from various covenants.
> 4. Use the covenant paradigm as a hermeneutic for understanding and interpreting scripture.

5. Evaluate his/her own personal participation in covenant relationship with God.

A set of *weekly*[1] learning objectives connected to this same course could be:

Weekly Objectives – Week #1:

1. The student will be able to define covenant within a biblical context. (Mapped to #1 and #2 above)

2. The student will be able to describe the particulars of a covenant relationship in broad categories. (Mapped to #2 above)

3. The student will be able to explain how the covenants provide a unifying theme for understanding how God has and is working with humankind. (Mapped to #3 above)

As you can see, the course objectives #1, 2, and 3 are touched upon in this week's objectives. Once the objectives are defined, then it is simply a matter of determining what should be assigned to accomplish those objectives and which in-class learning activities will best reinforce that learning.

Following these steps, it is possible to design a specific class session objectives, which focuses on achieving the broader objectives of the course. At first, this kind of work may seem to be too complicated or even too confusing, but after working with this process for a number of years and hundreds of faculty, I am convinced that this is one of the greatest needs of our educational system.

---

[1] Note this is only one week's learning objectives.

CHAPTER 4 - A TAXONOMY FOR LEARNING.

The original Bloom's taxonomy provided a way to evaluate the learning plan, as well as the learning accomplished. Bloom's hierarchy of levels of learning has been effectively guiding course development for decades and has had a profound effect upon the educational system. The descriptive terms of the taxonomy have made it possible to view learning using a graduated scale of lower level vs higher level thinking/learning. With the use of this tool, it has been possible to guide students into higher levels of learning through appropriate learning activities and assignments.

Anderson has revisited Bloom's taxonomy and made some modifications, which raise the effectiveness of the tool to a new level. In Bloom's original taxonomy, the major emphasis was on the cognitive functions. Within this domain, the descriptive terms identified the various levels of thinking. In Anderson's revision (Anderson, p.5), the taxonomy has been expanded into a two dimensional matrix, which connects the various levels in two dimensions: cognitive process dimension and the knowledge dimension.

In the cognitive dimension, there are six categories: remember, understand, apply analyze, evaluate and create. Think of the categories of the cognitive process dimension as column headings on a spreadsheet. In the knowledge dimension, there are four categories: factual, conceptual, procedural, and meta-cognitive. Think of the categories of the knowledge dimension as the rows of the spreadsheet.

	The Cognitive Process Dimension					
The Knowledge Dimension	1. Remember	2. Understand	3. Apply	4. Analyze	5. Evaluate	6. Create
A. Factual Knowledge	X					
B. Conceptual Knowledge						
C. Procedural Knowledge						
D. Meta-Cognitive Knowledge						

Each learning experience would then be able to be categorized on the knowledge dimension as factual, conceptual, procedural, or meta-cognitive (kind of a combination of the others) and correlated with one of the categories from the cognitive process dimension. For example, a learning experience could be both factual (knowledge dimension) and remembering (cognitive process dimension). An example would be learning vocabulary.

Although the U-CAT focuses on the cognitive process dimension and the categories associated with that dimension, regardless of the knowledge dimension, it is worth remembering that the categories of the knowledge dimension still affect learning.

Here are the levels, which Anderson has identified from the lowest to the highest level in the cognitive process dimension:

Remembering: Retrieving, recognizing, and recalling relevant knowledge from long-term memory.
Understanding: Constructing meaning from oral, written, and graphic messages through interpreting, exemplifying, classifying, summarizing, inferring, comparing, and explaining.
Applying: Carrying out or using a procedure through executing, or implementing.
Analyzing: Breaking material into constituent parts, determining how the parts relate to one another and to an overall structure or purpose through differentiating, organizing, and attributing.
Evaluating: Making judgments based on criteria and standards through checking and critiquing.
Creating: Putting elements together to form a coherent or functional whole; reorganizing elements into a new pattern or structure through generating, planning, or producing.

A well-designed course will take into account the academic status of the student (e.g. first year, sophomore, junior, senior, or graduate student), along with the complexity of the subject to be studied, and gradually lead the student to higher levels of learning. Keep in mind that some courses will be limited to the lower levels of learning by the nature of their subject, just as some will start at and move to ever-higher levels of learning for the same reason. I would argue that in every course there should be some movement toward higher levels of learning, whatever the starting point.

The relevance of this discussion comes when the cognitive dimension of the taxonomy of learning is associated with the curriculum in two ways.

First, how it affects the learning activities which occur in the classroom. While learning activities are the subject of another chapter, briefly they can be described as those activities occurring within the boundary of the classroom experience, which the instructor has designed to achieve student learning. By associating each of these activities with some level of the taxonomy of learning, it has the effect of guiding the teaching/learning process to insure higher levels of learning.

The second application has to do with the homework assigned for the course. The connection of the taxonomy of learning to assigned homework is often neglected, with the assumption that what is assigned actually achieves the goals necessary for learning to occur. What is typical, however, is that the assigned work simply follows the order presented in the book and falls mostly in the lower levels of the taxonomy. The result is that the homework assigned may actually do little to enhance the learning desired.

Therefore, understanding the taxonomy, and using it when considering both learning activities and homework assignments can have a profound effect upon the quality of the finished curriculum. As will be described later, the U-CAT provides space to associate both the learning activities and the homework assignments to different categories of the cognitive dimension, making it apparent at a glance their position on the taxonomy.

It also assists the course writer in determining whether the assignments and activities are actually achieving the envisioned goals for students completing the course. In this capacity the UCAT assists the course writer by identifying those activities or assignments, which need to be modified to strengthen the material to meet the desired effect.

CHAPTER 5 - ASSIGNMENTS

Every course will have assignments that have to be completed outside of class. The concern of this chapter can be divided into three areas:

- balance,
- relationship of assignments to course objectives, and
- relationship of assignments to the taxonomy of learning.

BALANCE

The balance of the amount of homework from week to week, as gauged by the time required to complete the assignments. Balance is typically overlooked by course developer or given only cursory thought, but has a big impact upon meeting the course objectives. A lack of reasonable balance is one of the most common complaints of students, i.e. "One week there are 20 hours of homework assigned and the next there are 5, why is that?" The most common reason this occurs is that the individual writing the course has not given sufficient thought about how the homework is balanced from week to week. Contributing to this problem is that there is rarely an established standard to use as a guideline. The U-CAT suggests a "load" based on the entry level of the student (e.g. first year, sophomore, junior, and senior) requiring more homework from those at higher levels to achieve higher levels of learning. The homework levels suggested in the U-CAT are:

a. 100 level courses = 7-9 hours/week

b. 200 level courses =8-10 hours/week

c. 300 level courses =9-11 hours/week

d. 400 level courses =10-12 hours/week

e. Masters level courses = 15-18 hours/week

f. Doctoral level course = 18+ hours/week

The rationale for this scale has to do with easing the student into the college experience while still establishing a standard of acceptable academic rigor. However, the important thing here is not the specifics of this scale but the establishment of a clearly defined scale, which can be used to guide the course development. By that I mean, your institution may adopt a completely different definition of work required for each level; the more important issue is that there IS a level of expectation.

Setting the standards, however, is only part of the process. There must also exist other definitions regarding the amount of time it takes for assignments related to reading, writing, research, project completion, etc. The U-CAT suggests standards in two areas, but each institution should consider further definitions, more on this in Chapter 9 on Calculating Seat-Time. The standards set by default in the UCAT are:

a. That assigned reading be calculated at 10 pages per hour and slightly less if, the material is highly technical.

      b.   That written work be calculated at two pages per hour.

The standards suggested above have been determined through experience working with students over a number of years. These may or may not coincide with your institution's experience or research. Here again, whether or not your institution adopts the same scale is not important. *What is important is that there is an accepted scale.* This allows the course writer to have the ability to evaluate assignments in relationship to the expectations of the program.

Using this scale, when 100 pages are assigned to be read, the time calculated for the average student to complete the reading would be approximately 10 hours; if you assigned 300 pages it could reasonably be expected to take 30 hours for the average student to complete that reading. Remembering the scale provided earlier in this chapter of the number of hours to be assigned outside of class, it is immediately apparent that there is a conflict between the standard and the assignment. What happens when this much reading is assigned is that students make value judgments based on what they feel is "fair" and the other commitments in their lives. If they believe they don't have that much time to devote to their homework, instead of reading the assigned pages, at best they will skim the material and at worst won't read it all.

Honestly, we probably did the same when we were in their shoes. Realistically, if you want the students to complete the assignments, they have to fit within reasonable boundaries. As a course writer and/or instructor, you may not like this and say "that's just too bad, the students will have to complete what has been assigned." Some students will complain and complete the work . . . most will not. This goes back to the basic educational philosophy: Subject Dissemination or Student Learning. If you need to assign 300 pages, you are better off assigning those pages to be "skimmed" for discussion in class, breaking them up and assigning different sections to groups to bring back a summary, or some other strategy, which keeps the assignment within the "reasonable" boundary. No one benefits from "over-assignment," and yet this is one of the most common errors of course writing.

I cannot overly emphasize the importance of this concept of "fair" within the mind of the average American student. Violation of that concept may be accepted occasionally, but an institution, which consistently violates it by assigning homework, which cannot be accomplished within the nebulous "fair" parameter, will suffer lower retention rates or a lower quality of student work, often accompanied by grade inflation to compensate, or both.

The U-CAT has space for the writer to list the assignments, in abbreviated form, along with the approximate amount of time it will require to complete those assignments. The times should be added in hour measurements, for instance, 1 hour, 1.3 hours, 1.6 hours, etc. The U-CAT automatically calculates the times for the week as well as averaged over the entire course so that the course writer can easily gauge whether or not there is an appropriate balance from week to week. An average of 9 hours a week for the course as a whole may seem reasonable, until you notice that the maximum for one week is 16 hours and the minimum in another week is only 4 hours. Ideally, the variation between the maximum and minimum should not exceed four hours and preferably not more than two hours. The goal is to balance the work assigned across all the weeks to fit the overall expectation for the course.

RELATIONSHIP OF ASSIGNMENTS TO COURSE OBJECTIVES

Another concern is how assignments are connected to the course objectives. *Homework must relate to the learning outcomes or it is a meaningless exercise.* That may seem obvious but I have reviewed enough curriculum to know that in some cases what has been assigned has nothing to do with the established learning outcomes. It might be a great learning exercise or a truly profound lecture; it might be a favorite assignment or topic for the Instructor. Regardless, if it does not clearly connect to the learning outcomes for that course, it should not be included.

The U-CAT allows space, on the same line as that used to calculate the time required to complete the course, to indicate which learning outcome(s) applies. By requiring each assignment to be linked to one or more learning outcomes, the curriculum becomes more focused in its ability to facilitate the learning for which it was intended and better able to guide the course writer in choice of assignments.

RELATIONSHIP OF ASSIGNMENTS TO TAXONOMY OF LEARNING

The third concern has to do with associating the assignments to the taxonomy of learning. The taxonomy of learning and its value for gauging assignments for their impact on learning was discussed in the previous chapter. There is another space on the U-CAT for making this association. By making the association between the assignment and the taxonomy, it becomes possible to determine the value of the homework as it relates to levels of critical thinking. It has been my experience that much of the homework assigned beyond the reading or watching a lecture, both of which are at the lower level of the taxonomy, is typically, written work. Written work which demands high time commitment but at lower levels of critical thinking it often results in simply regurgitating the reading. In some cases, it may even be defined as "busy work," which students deplore. The challenge which faces the course writer is how to be creative in making assignments, which accomplish the learning outcomes, as well as foster critical thinking, all within a reasonable period. I have included some suggestions below which may assist the course writer in thinking creatively about the type of assignments to be made.

Suggestions:

- For reading assignments:
  - The instructor writes a summary paper covering a larger reading assignment and assigns students to read this instead. Students can then be asked to:
    - Summarize the material in their own words.
    - Apply the information to a separate case
    - Create a quiz based on the reading
    - Suggest possible outcomes if some of the information was changed, e.g. in the battle of Gettysburg, would a change in the weather have affected the outcome? How? Why?
  - Assign smaller portions to different students or groups of students with the requirement to condense the reading into abstracts, which are posted to the course Learning Management System (LMS). If this method were used, pulling some questions randomly from this material for a quiz would be recommended.

- - Determine which part of the reading falls within the "irreducible minimum" and assign only those pages, using some of the suggestions below to augment the learning.
- While it is impossible to completely eliminate reading, nor should you, here are some alternative assignments to use to replace some of the reading assignment, if necessary to keep the homework within the prescribed time limits. Determine the "irreducible minimum" from the reading and alternate ways to achieve that learning. For instance:
  - watching a movie and writing a summary – or applying learning to the viewed material,
  - creating a playlist on youtube.com for students to watch,
  - have students create a playlist of a designated number of clips on youtube.com, which support the topic and explain how each one contributes to the topic.
  - have students create a youtube.com video themselves, demonstrating and/or explaining the concepts under discussion. Variation: once the student's video is posted, have other students analyze the video against a rubric. Some students could post the video one in the first week while others analyze, and then swap next week.
  - Assign an interview – e.g. when discussing history/sociology, interview someone in their 70's about their life as a child and how the world has changed.

- o Create a class blog and have students post related stories from the internet about the subject under discussion and make comments analyzing the article against a rubric provided by the instructor.
- o Create a class wiki and have students develop extensive hyperlinked documents around a central topic.
- O Assign the students to apply a principle to some aspect of their life and record the results in either a paper, vlogs, or blog. Variation, have them analyze the results, modify their approach and re-try, with a follow-up report.

Summary

Most courses are defined by the in class activities and the out of class assignments. Paying attention to the three considerations in this chapter will positively affect the quality of the curriculum for the course and facilitate student learning at higher levels of critical thinking.

CHAPTER 6 - LEARNING ACTIVITIES

Learning activities are those activities designed specifically to achieve student learning within the learning environment, either onsite, online (asynchronous), synchronous (but not geographically together), or some variation of all three. An example of these learning activities would include lecture, video, panel discussion, collaborative software, chat, video conferencing, etc. Learning activities are *the* heart of the teaching process. Here is where the fruit of the curriculum design has the potential to grow. Implementation of learning activities in instructional design is an expanding field of opportunity limited only by the imagination of the instructor and the instructional designer.

For traditional programs, class times vary from 45 – 90 minutes or more, 1-3 times a week. Many adult degree completion programs use a class format, which has the student in class once a week for 3-4 hours at a time. Online programs are typically asynchronous, although some have synchronous components. It is recommended that the learning activities during the on-ground class time be designed so that no learning activity exceeds 90 minutes total, and that even within a continuous learning activity, there be some kind of change of instructional style every 20-30 minutes to insure optimal learning. For instance if the instructor has scheduled a lecture which could last 90 minutes, there should be spaces within the lecture which are designed to allow the students to interact in a different way, e.g. discussion, brainstorming, etc., before going back to the lecture. For maximal learning, when classes extend past the 90-minute mark, it is also recommended that the students be given short breaks every 90 minutes. 90 minutes has been found to be the general limit for focused learning. Allowing short breaks at these points actually increases the likelihood of learning more than taking a longer break at the 2-hour mark. Thus, if an adult degree completion class started at 6:00PM, the first break would take place at 7:30PM for a few minutes and then again at approximately 9:00PM. An added benefit in this scenario is that by breaking at 9:00PM, and designing the last learning activity to be more interactive, students may be better engaged during that final hour than they might be otherwise. This is a big plus for adults who likely have been working all day and will be tired.

Similar to the chapter above, this area can be divided into three areas of concern, two of which correlate and one which is new.

The first concern is how the learning activities are connected to the course objectives. Just as homework must relate to the course objectives or it is a meaningless exercise, so too should the learning activities employed in the classroom/online environment connect to the learning outcomes. The U-CAT provides space to list the learning activity and to associate each activity with at least one learning outcome.

When discussing learning outcomes in an earlier section, I referenced the weekly learning objectives. Although the weekly learning objectives are not listed on the U-CAT, they should be a determining factor in the selection of the learning activities. The activities designed to promote learning should be *directly* associated with the weekly learning objectives and easily fit within one or more of the overall course objectives. When this kind of synchronicity occurs the likelihood of achieving the desired goal for the course is significantly increased. Faculty who adopt this model will find their ability to stay on track and focused will be greatly enhanced, which also contributes to student learning. Further, when this model is practiced in writing curriculum, those using the curriculum will find their task in staying on-track easier and produce better results overall.

The second concern has to do with associating the learning activities to the taxonomy of learning. There is a space on the U-CAT for making this association. By doing this, it becomes possible to determine the value of the learning activity as it relates to critical thinking. Although discussed more fully in the third concern below, the instruction style can significantly affect the level of critical thinking which is part of a learning activity. For example, although providing a wealth of information, the lecture would have to be considered, *in most cases,* as providing a lower level of critical thinking skills than would a classroom debate or class presentation. By making the association between the activity and the taxonomy of learning, the course writer can determine whether there is sufficient engagement, at appropriate levels, to facilitate the kind of learning desired.

The third concern has to do with associating the learning activities to the instructional style, which will be used during the time allocated for that activity. Again, there is a space on the U-CAT for making this association. Listed at the end of the U-CAT there appears a list of possible instructional styles which can be edited by the school to include others as desired. Those listed are:

- L = Lecture, which may or may not include visuals such as Power Point, pictures, graphics, objects, etc.
- M = Media, such as video, video clips, audio files, etc.
- C = Collaborative activities which may include interactive lectures in addition to other options. More on this is included later in this chapter.
- P = Presentations made by students, which can be in the form of a speech, augmented speech with PowerPoint or other visuals, or student demonstration.
- D = Demonstration made by the instructor or student, usually using some kind of physical process such as an athletic exercise, chemical experiment, step-by-step deconstruction of a passage of literature, working out a math problem on the whiteboard, etc.

By associating each learning activity with an instructional style it becomes easy to identify whether or not the course is being sensitive to adult learning pedagogy, which shies away from a predominately lecture model to one with a variety of instructional styles. An important benefit here is the ability to identify a specific instructional style. For instance, if an institution has set a standard that each course that students will have the opportunity to make an in-class presentation at least once during each course, it will be easy to scan the list of learning activities and the associated instructional styles to determine if that standard has been met. To do this simply scan the list of learning activities listed on the U-CAT to see if one has the designation "P" in the "instructional style" column.

SAMPLE LEARNING ACTIVITIES

There is no way any list of learning activities can be truly comprehensive. Some options are included below, some of which cross easily into both the on-site classroom and online.

Sample learning activities:

- Discuss case studies
- Computer simulations w/ teams
- Study groups/research projects
- Expert groups
- Issue debates
- Jeopardy w/ class material
- Games/Riddles
- Group create wiki
- Group creates PowerPoint & present
- Online threaded comment forums
- peer reviews of papers
- jigsaw (everyone does research & then come together to fit all parts together)
- role play
- pair share-discussion of application of visuals in pairs
- tie in life experiences & sharing how it applies to material

- Visual demonstration of theory
- Present themes w/ diff. mediums (sharing poetry, quotes)
- Brainstorming steps of a process…then order the steps as a group
- Determine the story behind a set of numbers: accounting
- Set a controversial topic…have students choose a point on the schema, then discuss
- Brainstorming
- Groups remember chapter contents from memory
- Collaborate on finding biblical principles in passage
- Brain + mapping/web
- Group engagement on story problems
- How do you do this task in different industries (shared experience)
- Write case studies
- "Zigzag"- rotate tables/each table has specific question to deal with
- Mock interviews/mock counseling
- Field trips

In our ever-changing environment, new collaborative activities and strategies are constantly being imagined and tested in the classroom. Instructional Designers and Instructors should always keep their eyes open for new ways to communicate with the current generation of students.

CHAPTER 7 - ASSESSMENT

The assessment section of the U-CAT asks that the course writer define what evidence will be used to "prove" the accomplishment of the course learning objectives. On the U-CAT, the course learning objectives, which are typed into the appropriate cells in Section A, will automatically duplicate in the Assessment Section with an additional column for describing the method of assessment. If well written, the course objectives will be measurable, i.e. it will be possible by some method to determine whether that objective has been accomplished. In some cases, the method of assessment will be contained within the course itself. For instance, the final paper required for the course may require the student to define and apply a specific learning theory, which was one of the course objectives. In this case, beside that objective, the course writer would simply enter "satisfied by final paper." There may be more than one way, which can evidence that the objective has been met, and there may be a measurement which may satisfy more than one objective. In the example above, the final paper may actually satisfy measurement of more than one of the learning objectives.

When possible, having the measurement tied directly to the course, as in the example above, is preferable; however, it is not required. In some cases the fact that it *can* be measured, does not necessarily mandate that it *be* directly measured. For instance, a course objective may state that upon completion of the course the student will be able to differentiate between two philosophical perspectives. This may be evidenced in a formal paper, or it may be assumed from the amount of instruction provided. If the evidence is in the paper, that should be listed as the measure of assessment, if it is assumed from the amount of instruction, the class session(s) where that subject was discussed should be listed in the assessment category.

In some cases, the assessment may lie outside the course completely. For instance, the passing of a certification exam given by an outside agency may relate directly to a course objective. In the same way a follow-up survey of an employer may also be a reasonable evidence of assessment, although more time consuming and difficult to track.

Whatever the method, it is important that each of the course objectives have an associated assessment. When writing the course, the author should discuss the assessment portion with the individual who assigned the course to be written for further insight about how the course fits into the larger academic program.

CHAPTER 8 - FAITH INTEGRATION

For institutions where there is an emphasis upon faith integration, the U-CAT includes a section, which may be used specifically for this purpose, or deleted if desired. Faith integration is somewhat of a nebulous concept, with different meanings for different institutions.

> "EXCEL's faith integration model is designed around a desire for an authentic interaction of faith and curriculum, allowing instructors the freedom to integrate their personal faith, recognizing the primacy of the educational purpose within the context of a Christian institution. The expression of this model will be the inclusion of optional faith integration suggestions to be included in the curriculum for each week. These suggestions will appear as a separate section prior to the week's learning activities and may be used, as the instructor feels appropriate. Instructors may also choose to use their own personal method of faith integration." (Taken from the report on the Task Force from Faith Integration in Huntington University, EXCEL, 2008).

Belhaven University modified their take on Faith Integration to be an intersection of the subject with a Christian Worldview. Built into each course at Belhaven, students are challenged to differentiate how the subject would be approached from secular and Christian worldviews, with the differences discussed and held up to scripture. Their curriculum development model includes the following statement: "All Belhaven University curriculum prepared for Online and Adult Studies will contain three solid touch-points for providing a Christian Worldview in every course. The three touch-points will be achieved through a) instruction, and b) assessment." The touch-points are associated with specific class sessions and include lecture, discussion posts, and an essay or a portion of the final paper.

At other institutions, the definition of faith integration is more vague, with many leaving the actual interpretation of what faith integration means to the course instructor, with no presence in the curriculum related to the issue.

Optimally, the course writer would suggest ways, either each week or at fixed points throughout the course, which would correlate with the learning objectives, assignments, and activities to provide a meaningful intersection between faith and learning. The UCAT includes space for noting such inclusions in the curriculum. Some examples of faith integration are listed below:

- Connect subject to a parable of Jesus.
- For nursing – in personal care use Jesus' actions.
- Evidence respect for different beliefs and cultures while contrasting with a biblical worldview.
- Follow-up on prayer requests.
- Use the Bible as a reference for specifics related to the subject.
- Pose a situation – e.g. Why did Jesus do "this."
- Pose the question, "why is the worldview on this point different that the Christian worldview (and how is it different?)."

- Discuss challenges the student(s) may have experienced in the business world related to a Christian worldview.
- Read scripture and compare it to the subject for that week.
- In an accounting class, ask what Jesus would do in the same situation (WWJD).
- In marketing, ask questions, which compare standards to biblical principles.
- Compare/contrast Christian vs non-Christian behavior in a given situation.
- Use a resource like the Maxwell Leadership Bible for topics relative to the subject.
- Personal examples of how faith has affected our lives.
- Current events can be used effectively to demonstrate a Christian worldview and/or lack thereof.

Note that prayer at the beginning of class is notably absent from this list. The rationale for this exclusion is that the use of prayer in this fashion too easily allows the instructor to "check off" the faith integration piece, without really addressing the intersection of the subject matter with a Christian worldview. Thus, instructors may or may not choose to begin a course with prayer but there should be purposeful thought given to the intersection of the secular and Christian worldview.

Anecdotally, most students when interviewed give instructors higher marks for faith integration when the class does begin with prayer, even when there is no additional effort made in this regard. Students also cite prayer at the beginning of class as an "expectation" of a Christian institution and that it provides a division, in most cases helpful, between their busy day and the beginning of class. While this perspective may seem like an argument for allowing prayer to stand as the fulfillment of the faith integration expectation, there is greater opportunity to affect our students than may simply beginning class with prayer. However, I would say from personal experience that doing so is beneficial to all concerned. The inclusion of a space in the U-CAT allows Faith Integration to be discussed at the very least.

CHAPTER 9 – CALCULATING SEAT TIME

The standard in use to calculate seat time for higher education at the time of this publication is the Carnegie definition. This definition, accepted by most regional accrediting bodies, states that one credit hour equals one 50 minute/week of in-class seat-time coupled with 2 hours/week out of class assignments, for a full standard semester (14-16 weeks, depending upon the institution. Doing the calculation for the full semester, this equates to 750 minutes for 15 weeks for the in-class portion (for the purpose of this example I'm using a 15 week semester), and 1,400 minutes for the 15 weeks for the out-of-class assignments/work. This totals 2,150 minutes for one college semester credit hour. Since most courses are 3 credit hours, that comes to 2,250 minutes for in-class and 4,200 minutes for out-of-class activities, or a total of 6,450 minutes (107.5 hours) for the semester.

If that is not confusing enough, consider the fact that most adult degree programs are condensed in some way, and online programs do not technically have an in-class experience and you can see potential problems in defining the seat hour. These kind of stressors are affecting the entire academy and it is likely that significant changes are forthcoming from the accreditors to take into account these and other variations, such as Competency Based Education (CBE).

Fortunately, in most cases the accreditors ask institutions to define a seat hour for their institution and then live by that definition, supported by examples. Here is where the UCAT and the UCATO can be invaluable tools for institutions who want to provide objective evidence of the appropriate rigor for their curriculum. The requirement to enter minutes related to assignments can quickly demonstrate to anyone reviewing the course that it either meets the standards set by the Institution or not.

Here is a sample credit hour definition from one university:

XXXXXX University Credit Hour Policy

Credit hours awarded for courses is determined by the faculty and academic administration in accordance with the mission and goals of XXXXXXX University. This determination is aligned with the Carnegie collegiate student credit hour, Federal definitions and requirements, and the standards, commission policies, and guidelines of XXXXXXXX, our regional accreditor. This credit hour policy guides the process for assigning credit hours for courses in the attainment of the XXXXXXX University's mission and goals.

Conforming to sound, commonly accepted best practices, the following statements are XXXXXXX University's working definition and principles for credit hour determination:

- The faculty oversees the content and quality of the curriculum and is responsible for the learning outcomes; therefore, it is the responsibility of the faculty to determine course credit hour valuations.

- The number of credit hours awarded for each course is determined on the basis of time spent in classroom instruction, outside class direct instruction, and outside class student work.
- One semester hour of credit is granted for the equivalent of 750 minutes of classroom instruction and 1500 minutes of outside class student work or 2250 minutes based on a combination of classroom instruction, outside class direct instruction, and outside class student work.
- Classroom instruction and outside class direct instruction times are equivalent for the purposes of credit hour valuations.
- Classroom instruction includes the formal class meeting, supervised labs, private instruction, or any similar instructional meeting between and instructor and one or more students.
- Outside class direct instruction includes student activities that:
  - Has a planned educational purpose or outcome
  - Is facilitated by an instructor or field supervisor (guided, monitored, or observed)
  - Is graded and documented
- Outside class direct instruction activities include but are not limited to
  - Online lectures or instruction (synchronous or asynchronous)
  - Video presentations, journal or blog writing
  - Chat rooms
  - Discussion boards
  - Field trips (which includes virtual field trips)
  - Group/team-based activities
  - Online test or quizzes
  - Video conferencing
  - Virtual labs
  - Supervised field experiences

- Outside of class student work includes course related activities that do not qualify as direct instruction. These activities include but are not limited to reading, writing, studying, preparing, practicing and researching.
- The ratio of classroom/outside class direct instruction and outside of class student work may vary depending on the course type. The ratio of outside of class student work serving in support of classroom/outside of class direct instruction is 2:1 (two minutes of outside of class student work supports one minute of classroom/outside class direct instruction.)
- The credit hour valuation is the same for all course formats, lengths, level, locations, and modes of delivery, which includes the traditional classroom, laboratory, online, electronic, private lessons, internships, practicums, independent study, senior thesis, or hybrid.
- The amount and level of credit hours awarded for a course will be determined according to these expectations and courses will be periodically evaluated to ensure that they meet or exceed these expectations.

Calculation of the minutes required for various activities as listed above can also be a challenge when attempting to fairly insert an appropriate number onto the UCAT or UCATO. The list below is included along with a recommended number of minutes for each activity.

Method / Modality	Unit Measured	Normal Time to Complete ** (in minutes)
Assigned activity (unsupervised)		actual time

Practice problems - complex	per problem	30
Practice problems - simple	per problem	15
Practicum (unsupervised)		actual time
Service learning (unsupervised)		actual time
Group presentation / panel / paper (group interaction)	per week, per project	180
Plot lab data in Excel		60
Portfolio development		240
PowerPoint presentation (e.g., student-created)	per slide	20
Speech / Lecture / Debate (practice before presentation)	per minute	9
Video presentation (e.g., student-created)	per min of finished video	30
Academic, Textbook, Literary Fiction - lower-level	per page	10
Academic, Textbook, Literary Fiction - upper-level	per page	15
Popular literature reading	per page	5
Sacred literature reading	per chapter	5
Science Lab reading	per lab	30
Walk/hike (unsupervised)		actual time

Electronic research (search, narrow results, analyze source)	per source	30
Group Wiki project	per entry - 250 words	30
Interview		actual time
Library research (search, narrow results, analyze source)	per source	60
Observation		actual time
Pre-lab exam studying	per lab exam	90
Pre-quiz studying	per quiz	60
Pre-test studying	per test	180
Analysis paper	per page - 250 words	60
Annotated bibliography	per annotation	20
Case study	per page - 250 words	60
Creative writing	per page - 250 words	60
Discussion board / Forum without direct instructor participation	per discussion	90
Genogram	per generation	120
Graphic org / Concept mapping / Mind map		90
Journal / Blog writing	per entry - 250 words	30

Lab notebook and report (pre- and post-lab)	per lab	60
Lesson / sermon / speech writing	per min of finished work	15
Peer-evaluation (e.g., of posted work)	per page - 250 words	45
Reflection paper	per page - 250 words	30
Report (video, field trip, tour, interview, lab, etc.)	per page - 250 words	30
Research / Term paper - lower-level	per page - 250 words	60
Research / Term paper - upper-level	per page - 250 words	90
Résumé and cover letter		120
Self-evaluation	per page - 250 words	25
Student course evaluation	per evaluation	15
Textbook chapter outline - lower-level	per chapter	60
Textbook chapter outline - upper-level	per chapter	90
Textbook chapter questions - lower-level	per chapter	60
Textbook chapter questions - upper-level	per chapter	90

Probably the most important point is that whatever definition is used by the Institution, it must be able to be defended as applicable for each of its various delivery modalities. In other words, say what you are going to do, then do it.

CHAPTER 10 - STEP-BY-STEP INSTRUCTIONS FOR USING THE CURRICULUM AUDIT

The U-CAT is a Microsoft Excel template, which is divided into sections that allows for the easy analysis of any piece of curriculum using predefined standards. To use the tool, simply open the template, "save as" the name of the course being audited and begin filling in the appropriate sections as described below.

SECTION A

In the appropriate spaces add the, course number, course number, course description, and course learning objectives. The course learning objectives will duplicate themselves in Section D.

SECTION B

Section B is where the in-class activities are listed:

Week	Learning Activities	SECTION B IN-Class Experience		
		Learning Outcomes	Bloom's	Style
1	I			
	II			
wk 1	III			
hmwk	IV			
hrs =	V			
0	VI			
	VII			
	VIII			

instance, you might replace 'I' with "Intro."

In the column marked "Learning Activities" you may replace the Roman numerals with a very brief identifier of a learning activity, or simply allow it to stand in representative of that which is found in the faculty guide. For

Week	Learning Activities	SECTION B IN-Class Experience		
		Learning Outcomes	Bloom's	Style
1	Intro			
	Lecture			
wk 1	Zigzag			
hmwk	Discussion			
hrs =	Video clp			
0	roundtable			
	VII			
	VIII			

In the column marked Learning Outcomes, you would connect the learning activity to one or more course learning outcomes from Section A, using the letter designation from that section. For instance, learning

activity 'IV' might be associated with learning outcomes 'A' and 'C.' It is possible that each learning activity might be associated with more than one learning outcome.

Week	Learning Activities	SECTION B IN-Class Experience		
		Learning Outcomes	Bloom's	Style
1	Intro	NA		
	Lecture	A		
wk 1	Zigzag	A		
hmwk	Discussion	AD		
hrs =	Video clp	BC		
0	roundtable	A		
	VII			
	VIII			

In the column marked "Bloom's," you would connect the learning activity to one or more of the taxonomy of learning levels discussed in a previous chapter. Those are also found at the end of the UCAT for easy reference. Note that if desired, this taxonomy may easily be replaced with another.

Week	Learning Activities	SECTION B IN-Class Experience		
		Learning Outcomes	Bloom's	Style
1	Intro	NA	NA	
	Lecture	A	A	
wk 1	Zigzag	A	C	
hmwk	Discussion	AD	B	
hrs =	Video clp	BC	A	
0	roundtable	A	C	
	VII			
	VIII			

Finally, in the column marked "Style" you would connect the learning activity to a particular style of instruction as discussed in a previous chapter. Again, these are found at the end of the UCAT for easy reference and may be replaced with a different list if desired.

In the case of "Style", there is usually only one letter of association, which is different from either of the columns for "Learning Outcomes" or "Bloom's" which may have more than one letter of association.

Week	Learning Activities	SECTION B Class Experience			IN-
		Learning Outcomes	Bloom's	Style	
1	Intro	NA	NA	L	
	Lecture	A	A	L	
wk 1	Zigzag	A	C	C	
hmwk	Discussion	AD	B	C	
hrs =	Video clp	BC	A	M	
0	roundtable	A	C	C	
	VII				
	VIII				

This is what the final completed table would look like.

SECTION C

SECTION C - OUT of Class Assignments						
Assignments	Reading	Writing	Research	Total	Learning Outcome	Bloom's
				0		
				0		
				0		

Section C is for recording the out-of-class assignments normally referred to as homework. The lines provided are not directly connected to same row data from Section B; however, it does connect in that it falls into weekly segments.

In the "Assignments" column, list in abbreviated form on separate rows each of the assignments for that specific week.

SECTION C - OUT of Class Assignments						
Assignments	Reading	Writing	Research	Total	Learning Outcome	Bloom's
Read Wilson pg 1-35				0		
Answer ? from Wilson on pg. 36				0		
				0		

In the next columns ("Reading," "Writing," "Research") insert a number in hours (e.g. 1 for one hour, 1.5 for one and one half hours, etc.) which represents the amount of time it would take for *an average student at the level matching the course number* to complete the assignment. There is a calculation guide at the end of the UCAT. This guide is discussed in a previous chapter and may be changed at the discretion of the institution.

The "Total" column will total the three columns into one number. The sum of this column, for this particular week is shown in the box in Section B to the left of the "Learning Activities" column. The average of all the weeks is shown above Sections B and C along with a maximum and minimum hours assigned. This allows an easy gauge of the homework load across the entire course.

SECTION C - OUT of Class Assignments					
Assignments	Reading	Writing	Research	Total	Learning Outcome	Bloom's
Read Wilson pg 1-35	3.5			3.5		
Answer ? from Wilson on pg. 36		2		2		
Write 1 pg paper		2		2		

In the column marked Learning Outcomes, connect the homework assignment to one or more course learning outcomes from Section A, using the letter designation from that section. It is possible that an assignment will be associated with more than one learning outcome.

SECTION C - OUT of Class Assignments						
Assignments	Reading	Writing	Research	Total	Learning Outcome	Bloom's
Read Wilson pg 1-35	3.5			3.5	A	
Answer ? from Wilson on pg. 36		2		2	A,C	
Write 1 pg paper		2		2	B	

In the column marked "Bloom's," you would connect the homework assignment to one or more of the taxonomy of learning levels discussed in a previous chapter. Again, these are also found at the end of the curriculum audit for easy reference.

SECTION C - OUT of Class Assignments						
Assignments	Reading	Writing	Research	Total	Learning Outcome	Bloom's
Read Wilson pg 1-35	3.5			3.5	A	A
Answer ? from Wilson on pg. 36		2		2	A,C	B,C
Write 1 pg paper		2		2	B	C

This what the completed section would look like.

SECTION D

This section provides the course writer the opportunity to demonstrate how each of the course objectives will be assessed. This is discussed more fully in a previous chapter.

SECTION E

This section provides the course writer the opportunity to provide suggestions for faith integration activities, which apply, to that week's learning objectives. This is discussed more fully in a previous chapter.

CHAPTER 11 - ONLINE VARIATIONS

Online instructional design represents some unique variations and so I have created an alternate version of the U-CAT, labeled the U-CATO to address these differences. The focus of this section will be to discuss some of the components of online instruction, which differ from the classroom, and how to design a course and audit it using the U-CATO to insure a quality. The course writer preparing material for an online course would be well advised to compliment this material with other curriculum design materials specifically designed for online instructors.

A significant variation of online versus the classroom model can be found in the learning activities. A purely online environment removes from the instructor's toolbox one of the most powerful tools – the ability to gauge student body language and garner non-verbal feedback to modify the flow of the instructional process. Because of this, both the curriculum and the instructor have to make extra effort at establishing a "presence" within the online course. Some activities, which help establish this presence, include:

- Introduction to the course in audio or video format.
- Weekly summary reinforces either on the discussion board, through an audio recording of the instructor, or a video clip.

- Audio feedback on assignments which can be inserted directly into MS Word files or the LMS
- Active involvement in a non-class related discussion forum and a willingness to share, appropriately, personal information.
- Make sure the Instructor's profile is updated in the LMS, including a recent picture.

Additionally, the online environment requires the instructor to prepare his/her materials significantly in advance of the actual class offering so that they can be uploaded into the course-site. This means much less flexibility/spontaneity than is found in the on-site classroom experience. For at least these two reasons many on-site instructors have not found teaching online to be a pleasurable experience. Some have estimated that building an online course takes approximately 180 hours from start to finish, all of which has to be completed before the class even starts.

Yet, there are tremendous benefits for those who can accept these boundaries. One of the benefits is the greater demand on students to become actively involved in the learning process through the discussion boards. Part of the expanded interaction comes because of stated requirements for posting, however, there can be seen in most online courses an amazing "blooming" of some students who would normally sit quietly through an on-site course. This kind of experience can be equally as exciting for the online instructor as the classroom buzz is for the on-site instructor.

So, what does an online course look like and how should you think about constructing an online course? Regardless of your learning platform, there are several components, which can be used to construct a dynamic online experience for students, which equals if not surpasses, the on-site experience. Before we look at these components, we need to go over some basic vocabulary:

- Learning Management System (LMS) - The LMS is commonly an institutional decision based on a variety of factors such as cost, bandwidth, support, etc. Most LMS systems work pretty much the same so if you learn one system it probably would not take long to gasp the functioning of a different system. These LMS systems allow students to login to a closed system and onto a specific course-site, which contains all the bits and pieces related to a specific course. Most of these bits and pieces are going to come from the course writer, but there may be some standard pieces, which have been established by the institution to be present in all course sites. An example would be a generic discussion forum for students to "discuss" topics unrelated to the course.

- Synchronous – courses, which are synchronous, are courses in which everyone is present at the same time. Most online courses do not fit this description since one of the benefits of online instruction is the ability to work it around different work/life commitments. However, online courses may have a synchronous component, which may take the form of a video conference at scheduled points throughout the course. These synchronous events may or may not be required, are typically recorded, and available for students to review as needed. In online's early days synchronous was a standard part of the model using either chat or video conferencing. That model gradually was discontinued in favor of the asynchronous model, largely due to complications in geography and internet infrastructure, which simply could not handle the bandwidth necessary for a quality synchronous experience. Although the bandwidth issues are largely in the past, asynchronous is still the most common model for online courses.

- Asynchronous – courses, which are asynchronous, are courses in which students and instructors interact regularly throughout a fixed period, but not necessarily at the same time. In an asynchronous course, the instruction may be broken into weeklong segments, but there are few restrictions on when to participate in the course experience. In the asynchronous environment students and instructor will rarely be "online" at the same time but can still contribute to a meaningful interaction. The asynchronous format is perfect for geographically dispersed participants who can login to the course site at the times and places that fit their schedule.

- Static – online courses which are static have little or no requirements for instructor/student interaction and perform very much like stand-alone independent study, or what used to be called correspondence courses. These courses are best used for training purposes and can be quite effective in providing training for specific skills or tasks.

- Hybrid: Refers to courses within a program that consists of entire courses delivered either fully online or fully on-ground, however, both types of courses may make up the program. For example, course XX1 is only offered online, while XX2 is only offered on-ground[2].

---

[2] Hybrid and Blended terms are often switched by different institutions or combined in some way or confused with the Augmented format. There is little clarity within the Academy as a whole on how they terms are used

- Blended: Courses contain both online and on-ground components, which reduces the number of on-ground sessions. For example, the course may meet on weeks 1, 3, 5, & 7 on ground and weeks 2, 4, 6, and 8 through online.

- Augmented: On-ground courses, which include aspects of online course delivery, e.g. discussion boards, but does not necessarily affect the number of on-ground sessions, nor the length of the on-ground session.

- Virtual Synchronous (VS): Refers to courses, which are delivered entirely through video conference. VS courses have aspects of both the on-ground and online delivery modalities. In a typical design, these courses would meet at regular intervals, e.g. weekly, on the same date and at the same time. The VS course would be augmented by use of an LMS to carry the load of much of the instructional content. The advantage of the VS course is the regular presence of a live instructor and the interaction with other students in the "virtual" classroom, while offering some of the flexibility of the online course.

Some of the components used in creating an online class are:

- Discussion forum – the discussion forum is also known as a threaded discussion because it ties or "threads" online posts[3] together so that it is recognizable as a conversation. This "tying" or "thread" is found in the

---

[3] "Posts" in the context of an online discussion form mean the typed entries students make in response either to the question or in reply to another student's post. Posts can be done in real-time while connected to the internet or composed offline using a word processor and then pasted into the discussion board.

common subject line and posting structure which cascades under an initial comment or question.

- o Discussion forums are the most prominent feature of online courses. In a discussion forum, the instructor posts a question to the course site and students respond to that question and to each other's posts, creating a virtual discussion. Since this is usually happening asynchronously, students may be posting at any time day or night throughout the week and have the luxury of taking time to think through their response and even research supporting documentation, which can also be a stated requirement of the initial question. For instructors the discussion forums are the source of the greatest opportunity to gauge learning through reading the students' posts. They can also be the bane of an instructor's existence since every student will post to every question and often enter into full discussions, requiring significant faculty time to read and evaluate.

- o Variations to the discussion forum can include the possibility of blocking other students from viewing other student posts until they have made their initial post. The advantage of this variation is that it requires each student to fully answer the question without being tempted to paraphrase another student's post or simply say "ditto."

- o Discussion forums work well in either low or high bandwidth scenarios.

- o There are two keys to effectively using the discussion forum to facilitate student learning.

- The first is to construct good questions. The components of a good question include:
    - Being stated in such a way that it requires several lines to adequately answer the question.
    - Being provocative toward encouraging students to think critically.
    - Opens the door for further inquiry
- The second is to have clearly stated expectations for student responses. Some examples of expectations are:
    - Require the answer to be a certain number of lines or words in length.
    - Require the answer to include a link to a supporting web document, which applies to the subject.
    - Require that students make their initial post early enough in the week that other students can reply.
    - Require students to reply meaningfully to other students for full credit.

- Lectures – Lectures for online courses are not the same as classroom lectures and take many forms. In all of these cases, the major distinctive of the online course is that this material is prepared before the course even begins and is posted to the course site. Making last minute corrections can be done, but can be technically complicated and often causes confusion. Some of the variations are:

- o Audio files (mp3) which the instructor records and the student can download and listen to in a variety of ways.
- o Video files which the instructor or SME records and uploads to the course site. Video files can also be used as an introduction to a topic with additional connected assignments or as an example of the principle under discussion.
- o White papers which the instructor writes for the student to read.

Depending on the amount of media, lectures can work well in either low or high-bandwidth.

- Media Clips – these can be assigned from a variety of sources and used to introduce discussions, form the basis of a quiz, etc.
- Quizzes/Tests – these are easily constructed for the online course site and can have great benefit if used wisely. An example would be to have each week be introduced with a pre-quiz, which is not counted toward the grade. If the pre-quiz is successfully passed at whatever level the instructor sets, then the program can unlock the key for taking the end-of-week quiz. Online quizzes can be in almost any format. If clearly pre-defined answers are identified (e.g. multiple choice, true/false, short answer, matrix, ranking, etc.), the course site will automatically grade the quiz and post it to the course gradebook. Unless there is a media component to the quiz/test, these generally work in either low or high bandwidth scenarios. In many cases, an institution will employ third-party vendors to insure quizzes/tests are completed with integrity.

- Glossary – just like it sounds but with an online benefit, glossaries are areas of the course site to which students can be assigned to contribute. The resource then becomes available to the whole class.

- Wikis – a wiki is a group workspace, which can be used for a variety of purposes such as developing a group paper, building a group knowledge base (e.g. Wikipedia), etc. The use of wikis is beginning to be recognized as one of the stronger resources for online learning components since it is a highly collaborative space. Problems associated with wikis usually revolve around that which makes it the greatest benefit – i.e. its collaborative nature.

- Collaborative workspaces – Similar to Wikis is the collaborative work spaces now found in products like Google Drive and Microsoft Office 365. These tools and other like them allow students to work on the same document, spreadsheet, or presentation at the same time from geographically diverse locations. This makes team projects and collaboration possible in an online environment.

- Questionnaires and Surveys – since the course site can summarize this data on the fly, these can be useful tools for getting an understanding of student experience/opinion on various course related topics.

- Assigned homework – usually in the form of reading textbook and providing written answers to specific questions. This can also include research using the Institution's digital resources and writing papers. In most cases this type of assignment is completed by the student offline and submitted to a class "dropbox" (digital storage center) and can be a single file or multiple files.

- Textbook websites are becoming more and more popular and some online courses take advantage of these resources to augment some aspect of the course.

- Open Educational Resources (OER) – OER is expanding in availability. These resources are typically free, or nearly so, to students and faculty and available in digital format, primarily, which makes them ideal for online. OER is growing in popularity, but has not fully reached its potential, mostly due to diversity of subject, lack of peer review for quality, and fewer, if any, instructor resources.

- Augmented Instructor Resources – These resources are now readily available for almost any textbook and provide the instructor with a wealth of additional materials to supplement their teaching. These include, but are not limited to: Slide sets, suggested video clips, worksheets, lecture notes, etc.

USING THE U-CATO TO HELP DEVELOP AND AUDIT THE ONLINE COURSE

Use of the U-CATO for online curriculum is the same as for the in-class curriculum as described in the previous chapter for Sections A, D, and E and I will not repeat this information here[4]. The major departure is in Sections B and

---

[4] In developing the online course, the same process described under "Weekly Objectives" found on page 17-20 can be followed with great effect. Although the assignments and activities may vary due to the nature of the online environment, the actual process remains basically the same, i.e. what assignments will facilitate learning which accomplishes the weekly objectives and which activities will best reinforce that learning.

C. Since there is no discernable separation from the "In-class experience" and "Out of class assignments", these two sections have been combined for the U-CATO and labeled Section BC. Another variation is the time expectations listed on the U-CATO for the various levels. This change has been made because the amount of assigned homework measured for the U-CAT did not include time spent in class (seat time), which has to be part of the overall calculation for the U-CATO. The table below describes the difference proposed between the two tools. Keep in mind these time allocations may easily be adjusted by the institution according to its own guidelines.

	On-site course - weekly expectations for completion of Homework (does not include seat time in class)	Online course - weekly expectations for completion of all work
Freshmen 100 level courses	7-9 hours	8.5 – 10.5 hours
Sophomore 200 level courses	8-10 hours	9.5 – 11.5 hours
Junior 300 level courses	9-11 hours	10.5 – 12.5 hours
Senior 400 level courses	10-12 hours	11.5 – 13.5 hours
Graduate >400 level courses	11-13 hours	12.5 – 14.5 hours

Keeping in mind the various components for online courses describe briefly above, the next step is to determine which of those will best facilitate student learning within the context of the weekly learning objectives. The U-CATO's role is to allow the writer/instructor to evaluate how well their course accomplishes:

1. The goals for balance (i.e. time spent per week).

2. How each week addresses the overall course objectives?

3. The rigor of the assignments/activities using a learning taxonomy.

An example of the U-CATO used for Week #1 for Biblical Covenants is shown below. Note that calculating time for reading and responding to discussion forum questions may be difficult to calculate.

Week		Assignments/Activities	Listening/ Reading	Writing	Other	Total	Learning Outcome	Bloom's
		SECTION BC - list times in hourly increments or portions thereof (e.g. 90 minutes = 1.5 hours)						
1	I	Introduction			.75	.75	NA	NA
	II	Read Ch. 1 / Answer ???	1.2	1.5		2.7	A	B
wk 1	III	Read Article & Answer ??	.5	1		1.5	B	B
	IV	Read Lecture L1L1	1			1	A	A
hrs =	V	Read Lecture L1L2	1			1	A	B
10.45	VI	Discussion #1		1.5		1	NA	NA
	VII	Discussion #2		1.5		1.5	A	B
	VIII	Discussion #3		1.5		1.5	A	B

For more on this check out Chapter 9 – Calculating Seat Time.

You can see that the expected time commitment for this example for the week's instructional experiences is projected to be 10.45 hours. The various columns show how the time is distributed The Learning Outcome column identifies each of the activities as they relate to the learning outcomes for the course – again, this forces the developer to make sure of the alignment of all the activities toward the goal for that course. The Bloom's column also helps the developer consider their assignments and expectations in light of critical thinking standards.

CHAPTER 12 - CONCLUSION

Writing quality curriculum takes time and requires the author to bring into balance several different components. The U-CAT or U-CATO and this guidebook will provide a useful tool to assist in developing superior curriculum.

BIBLIOGRAPHY

Anderson, Lorin W., David R.Krathwohl, Peter Airasian, Kathleen Cruikshank, Richard Mayer, Paul Pintrich, James Raths, Merlin Wittrock. <u>A Taxonomy for Learning, Teaching, and Assessing: A Revision of Bloom's Taxonomy of Educational Objectives.</u> New York: Longman, 2001.

Barkley, Elizabeth F., K. Patricia Cross, Claire Howell Major. <u>Collaborative Learning Techniques: A Handbook for College Faculty.</u> San Francisco: Josey Bass, 2005.

Collison, George, Bonnie Elbaum, Sarah Haavink, Robert Tinker. <u>Facilitating Online Learning: Effective Strategies for Moderators.</u> Madison, WI: 2000, 2000.

Elbaum, Bonnie, Cynthia McIntyre, and Alese Smith. <u>Essential Elements: Prepare, Design, and Teach Your Online Course.</u> Madison, WI: Atwood Publishing, 2002.

Gibson, Chere Campbell. <u>Distance Learners in Higher Education: Institutional Responses for Quality Outcomes.</u> Madison, WI: Atwood Publishing, 1998.

Pallof, Rena M., Keith Pratt. <u>Building Learning Communities in Cyberspace.</u> San Francisco: Josey Bass, 1999.

Richardson, Will. <u>Blogs, Wikis, Podcasts, and Other Powerful Web Tools for Classrooms.</u> Thousand Oaks, CA: Corwin Press, 2009.

Richlin, Laurie. <u>Blueprint for Learning: Constructing College Courses to Facilitate, Assess, and Document Learning.</u> Sterling: Stylus, 2006.

Vella, Jane. <u>Taking Learning to Task: Creative Strategies for Teaching Adults.</u> San Francisco: Jossey-Bass, 2001.

Wilkinson, Bruce. <u>The 7 Laws of the Learner: How to Teach Almost Anything to Practically Anyone</u>. Sisters, Oregon: Multnomah Press, 1992.

Made in the USA
Coppell, TX
24 January 2022

72248629R00052